Do You Believe in Ghosts?

Fortune-tellers, Séances, Mediums, and More!

Other books in the sunscreen series:

feeling freakish?
how to be comfortable in your own skin

just us girls
secrets to feeling good about yourself, inside and out

my parents are getting divorced
how to keep it together when your mom and dad are splitting up

sex explained
honest answers to your questions about guys & girls,
your changing body, and what really happens during sex

when life stinks
how to deal with your bad moods, blues, and depression

drugs explained
the real deal on alcohol, pot, ecstasy, and more

don't be shy
how to fit in, make friends, and have fun—even if you weren't born outgoing

dealing with mom
how to understand your changing relationship

dealing with dad
how to understand your changing relationship

weighing in
how to understand your body, lose weight, and live a healthier lifestyle

all about adoption
how to deal with the questions of your past

flying solo
how to soar above your lonely feelings, make friends, and find the happiest you

walking tall
how to build confidence and be the best you can be

Do You Believe in Ghosts?

Fortune-tellers, Séances, Mediums, and More!

By **Martine Laffon**
Illustrated by **Martin Matje**
Edited by **Kate O'Dare**

sunscreen

Library of Congress Cataloging-in-Publication Data

Laffon, Martine.
Do you believe in ghosts? : fortune-tellers, séances, mediums, and more!
/ by Martine Laffon ; illustrated by Martin Matje.
p. cm.
Includes bibliographical references and index.
ISBN 978-0-8109-8356-4 (Harry N. Abrams, Inc. : alk. paper)
1. Occultism—Juvenile literature. 2. Parapsychology—Juvenile literature.
I. Matje, Martin. II. Title.

BF1411.L25 2009
130—dc22
2008028309

Translated by Natalie Kone

Book series design by Higashi Glaser Design

Printed and bound in China
10 9 8 7 6 5 4 3 2 1

Amulet Books are available at special discounts when purchased in quantity
for premiums and promotions as well as fundraising or educational use.
Special editions can also be created to specification. For details, contact
specialmarkets@hnabooks.com or the address below.

HNA ▌▐▐▐▐
harry n. abrams, inc.
a subsidiary of La Martinière Groupe
115 West 18th Street
New York, NY 10011
www.hnabooks.com

contents

Is it really possible to communicate with dead people? Throughout history people have certainly tried, and there are many different approaches. In the mid-nineteenth century, a philosophical school of thought called *spiritism* became very popular in France. The spiritists believed in God, but were very interested in the relationship between the human world and the spirit world. They felt that communication with spirits was possible. Spiritism was not a religion, and there was no scientific proof that its theories were true, but it's still interesting to learn about today. Interest in paranormal and parascientific phenomena became trendy in many places around the globe, but this book will focus primarily on the ideas of the French spiritists. Many of these ideas might seem out of this world, so just remember to read these pages in the *spirit* of fun!

The spirit world has continued to interest, thrill, or frighten people so much that it's still a popular topic. Just think of all the movies, books, and TV shows that deal with the subject—who wouldn't be curious? Stories of table-turning, automatic writing, and Ouija boards haunt middle schools and high schools.

At slumber parties, many a spirit gets invited over. But is practicing spiritism just chanting goofy phrases in a dark bathroom? What do we want to know by communicating with spirits? And more important, who are these so-called spirits? What do they want to tell us: our future, answers to test questions, the name of next season's *American Idol* winner . . . ? And is it dangerous to talk to them?

Couldn't thinking that certain coincidences are messages from the spirit world make you crazy? Does everything we observe around us have a rational and scientific explanation? Should we look to science or religion when we have questions about death and belief in an afterlife? When we die, will our soul or spirit just disappear, or can we come back to visit? When you think about how huge these questions are, you can see why the idea of spirits and the spirit world is so compelling. This book will share some ways of dealing with these questions and uncertainties. The desire to connect with the spirit world isn't crazy or evil—everyone has curiosity about the unknown.

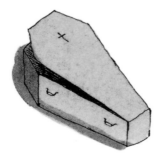

famous
mediums

what is
a spirit?

where do
spirits hang
out?

what about god?

PAGING ALL SPIRITS!

are you a good medium?

what is a
spirit?

One of the approaches to thinking about and communicating with the spirit world is called spiritism. Spiritism is a doctrine founded on "the existence, the manifestations, and in it the teachings of spirits." According to this doctrine, the afterlife exists, and in it you can enter into contact with spirits. But how can you communicate with them if they're not visible? How do you even know if they are there or what to look for? For the spiritists, humans are composed of three elements: the soul, the physical body, and the perispirit. The soul, a person's spiritual core, is immaterial and immortal. It thinks, wants, and feels all sorts of emotions, but it doesn't have a shape. The physical body is easy to understand—it's what you see when you look in the mirror. The perispirit (the origin of the word is Greek: *peri*, "around," and *spiritus*, "spirit") is a more complicated idea. For the spiritists, the perispirit is a coating that protects the soul and keeps it firmly in its physical body. Imagine a peanut; now imagine that the outer shell is your physical body. When you crack it open, the nut still has a thin, papery skin protecting it. That skin is the perispirit, sort of an envelope for the soul. This envelope is also what gives the soul its "shape," but we'll get to that in a second.

how spirits
are different

As long as you're alive, everything's fine! The three elements—soul, physical body, and perispirit—stick together and are impossible to separate. But, at the moment of death, everything gets complicated. As is so often the case, right? According to the spiritists, the body decomposes and the soul regains its liberty but is still wrapped in the perispirit. Here's where the soul's shape comes into play: the perispirit retains the human characteristics that were present in the physical body, both the good and bad. If you were a great person or a jerk before death, you'll probably be the same afterward . . .

unless you become reincarnated and your soul has the time to get in better shape and attain some new wisdom. There's always room for improvement!

So a spirit is a combination of a soul and its perispirit, which have been liberated from their physical body by death.

If soul + perispirit = spirit, spirits must therefore be human beings liberated from their bodies by death. For believers in spiritism, the world is chock-full of spirits just waiting to get in touch with us. It is important to keep in mind that for a spiritist, there is nothing supernatural about this desire to chat. Spirits are just people who no longer have their physical bodies but are clothed in only their perispirits. These spirits are hanging around waiting to be reincarnated so they can learn and progress through other existences. If you've ever been stuck at the airport because of long delays, you can empathize with a desire for conversation to pass the time.

Spiritists believe in God, creator of the universe, in the soul, and in its immortality. Influenced by Christianity, spiritists firmly believe in loving thy neighbor as much as thyself. So spiritists think that if a spirit wants to get in touch and makes a friendly overture, why not respond? After all, they are still thy neighbors, even if they're only wearing their perispirits!

where do spirits
hang out?

They're the homeless of the spiritual world. The spirits of those you've loved, but also of people who've been dead for thousands of years, all share your space. This isn't so obvious since even if they still possess their human form, thanks to the perispirit, they are invisible, and usually you can't detect their presence. But, according to spiritists, they're very much there, around you. They observe you and can occasionally advise you, help you, trigger a reaction, or influence your dreams without you even knowing it. But don't get too excited: even if they really like you, they won't whisper the solution to an especially tough SAT question. Spiritists believe that the

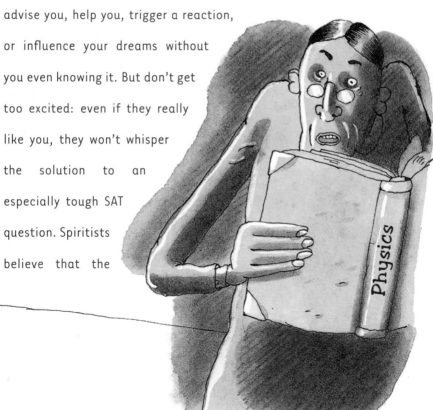

spirit's main focus is to show that death is not the end and that a spiritual presence and energy persists even when our physical bodies are gone. This is a big message to get across, so you can understand why they aren't preoccupied with helping on exams or providing insight on crushes. That would be great, though . . .

can you
talk to them?

How do you know which spirit you're speaking to? Spiritists agree that all spirits aren't necessarily smart, wise, or as fun as a barrel of monkeys. Some spirits should be avoided completely. To figure out what kind of spirit they were dealing with, spiritists developed a three-level scale that they said was revealed by the spirits themselves. At the very bottom are the rather rotten spirits of the third order. There you find impure and wicked spirits and the occasional evil genius, but also little spirits (sprites and pixies), spirits who are often proud and jealous, and neutral spirits, who are still drawn to life on earth. The conversations of these spirits tend to be dull and can sometimes even be crude.

Next come the good spirits of the second order, who, according to spiritists, are close to God. Wise, intelligent, and benevolent, they are superior spirits and are committed to giving spirits an excellent name. They are also friendly and will gladly agree to communicate with those who are looking for answers in good faith. At the very top of the scale is the first order of spirits, who are intellectually and morally superior to all other spirits. Angels or archangels, they are God's messengers: they command inferior beings, assist people in distress, and help them to do good. Not surprisingly, these spirits prefer to be consulted on large issues only; they don't like to sweat the small stuff. Using this scale, it is easier to know whom you're dealing with, and most of all, when attempting to communicate you can put in a request. One superior spirit, coming up!

spiritism:
is this a new idea?

Yes and no. Along with attempts to turn any random thing into gold, learning to tell the future, or divination, has been one of humankind's greatest preoccupations. Every culture has tried it, one way or another, and some of the methods they used are hard to believe today. For instance, during antiquity, necromancy was a popular form of divination, especially with certain Greek societies. What's necromancy, you ask? Basically it means consulting the dead to learn about the future. On the surface that's not so strange—many cultures pray to their ancestors—but necromancy took it a gag-inducing step further. The principle was simple and outrageous: Offer the same sacrifices to a dead body as you would to the gods. Specially trained priests sacrificed animals and dripped warm blood onto a cadaver in the hope that the spirit of the dead person could ask the gods questions about the future and report back to the priests. The priests would then announce that they had received a message and would interpret it. Since the priests needed silence and almost total darkness, they worked in caves, lived on the remnants of the sacrificed animals, and thought themselves to be learning secret or future things from the mouths of the dead. Learning secrets or not, it seems like a pretty gloomy job.

In America, the first burst of interest in spiritism, as we are talking about it here, really came about in 1847, in Hydesville, New York. The Fox family, with their daughters, Margaret and Katherine, moved into a small farmhouse that had a reputation for being haunted. After several months, they started hearing rapping. Not like hip-hop, but sharp knocking sounds! In March of 1848, the sounds were so loud that they shook the walls and floorboards. They became so overwhelmingly intense that Katherine, the younger of the two girls, amused herself by clapping her hands in response. Mrs. Fox, without really knowing why, then spoke to the noise: "Count until twenty!" They heard twenty raps. She then said to it: "If you are human, rap once." Complete silence. "If you are a spirit, rap twice." Two raps were heard. With the help of their neighbor, the Foxes created an alphabet so that the spirit could communicate. The spirit obligingly rapped each letter of his name. That's how they learned that it

was Charles B. Rosma, who was murdered by a previous tenant and buried in the basement. They proceeded to dig up the basement, where human bones were discovered. That seemed to make a very good case for the possibility of communication with the afterlife, although it also raises lots of questions.

the guy
who started it all

The news spread across America, and the Fox sisters became famous overnight. Just a few years later, in 1852, the first spiritism conference took place. As early as 1854, there were three million American practitioners of spiritism, along with one hundred thousand people calling themselves mediums. Mediums are the "middlemen" for spirits, sharing their messages with the living and summoning them to communicate. The phenomenon wasn't only American, either: Great Britain, Belgium, Austria, and Prussia also became involved in the spiritist movement. By 1853, Strasbourg and Paris were affected by the craze, as were most of the big cities in France and eventually even the French countryside. The table-turning epidemic spread everywhere. So what exactly is table-turning? Table-turning is just like using a Ouija board, only it's the table that moves in response to questions. In 1854, Hyppolite Léon Rivail (1804–1869), a man from Lyon, France, felt

ph1

invested with a mission: to write down the tenets of the spiritist doctrine as the spirits transmitted them to him. He wrote *The Spirits' Book* in 1857 under the pseudonym Allan Kardec. The book was such a blockbuster that it was reprinted fifteen times during the author's life.

what about
God?

So who was this guy Kardec? And how did someone interested in chemistry and mathematics come to be socializing with spirits? Since he was a kid, Hyppolite Léon Rivail was fascinated by magetism, somnambulism (also known as sleepwalking), and hypnosis. At age twenty-eight, after having studied in Lyon and Switzerland, he married and founded a small school with his wife that employed new teaching methods. But the school went bankrupt. Rivail continued, however, to teach classes in physics and astronomy for free in his home. In 1854 he attended spiritist séances and attempted to logically

understand what was happening. Convinced by the mediums' revelations, he spent the last fifteen years of his life committed to the spiritist doctrine. On March 31, 1869, after having officially changed his name to Allan Kardec, the father of spiritism died. He is buried at Père-Lachaise Cemetery in Paris, and his tomb is always covered with flowers, a testament to the strong belief he inspired and to the loyalty of his followers. With *The Spirits' Book*, the ideological basis of spiritism was spelled out: It is a doctrine that is opposed to materialism and that supports a belief in God, in the soul, and in the survival of the soul after death. It doesn't offer proof of the existence of spirits: The revelation of the doctrine by the spirits themselves is, for spiritists, the proof. "You who deny the existence of spirits, fill the void they occupy, and you who laugh, dare then to laugh at the works of God and His omnipotence." (Allan Kardec, *The Spirits' Book*).

are you a
good medium?

If all of this has convinced you and you are ready to do some communicating, the next question is, are you a good medium? How do you know if you are? If you decide to try, keep in mind that none of this is dangerous. Nothing bad is going to happen, but you may end up with a headache from concentrating or you may get spooked when your cat puts his paw on your foot. Many people feel they have some sensitivity, whether it is to spirits or knowing the phone is going to ring before it does. Spiritists believe that dedication to the pursuit of communication will make up for any lack of natural talent in communicating with spirits.

Before you decide to chuck that internship and become a full-time medium, be warned that mediums are not magicians; they can't produce miracles or make people disappear. Nor can you judge a medium by his or her cover—there is no physical "type" that corresponds to sensitivity to the spirit world. Some spiritists even say you can cultivate your talent as a medium by eating well, not overdoing caffeine, and generally working to develop your intellectual capabilities! Through this work you will become more attuned to those better spirits of the higher orders. Limiting caffeine is essential—what you think might be the vibrations of a spirit moving through you could just be that ninth Diet Coke.

the different methods
of communication

Just as there are all sorts of spirits, there are almost as many types of mediums. Some even have the ability to smell spirits. No matter what approach the mediums use, they can only reach out to the spirit; it is up to the spirit to decide if it wants to respond.

If you are thinking about specializing, here are three of the most common types of mediums:

- Mental mediumship involves the medium receiving messages from the spirit world telepathically. This is the most familiar form, one you've seen in a ton of movies and TV shows.

- Trance mediumship involves the medium entering an altered state of consciousness, often through hypnosis. While the medium is in the trance, the spirit "speaks" through the medium. This form was very popular in the late nineteenth century.

- Physical mediumship allows the spirit to communicate by moving things around or making noise. "Knock three times if you can hear me, spirit."

Some followers of spiritism think that it isn't necessary to ask questions and believe that, out of respect for the spirit, it's best to let it talk spontaneously. But questions have the advantage of sparking a discussion. No matter what, the spirit will talk only if it is in the mood. It may also decide to ask *you* a question: "What do you want? Ask me and I will respond!" It might ask you to be more specific in your thoughts or be more attentive. When a spirit talks, for goodness' sake remember your manners and don't interrupt!

The spiritists think superior spirits are easily offended. Avoid asking them lame questions or they'll get annoyed. What's a lame question? As tempting as it is, don't ask who'll win the Kentucky Derby or if your lab partner would go out with you; what would amuse those rude and crude inferior spirits runs the risk of irritating a high spirit. Moreover, spirits themselves say: "A stupid question deserves a stupid answer!" What a tough crowd!

If the spirits don't respond to you, it might be because they find the question uninteresting or way too specific. What does that mean, you ask? Shouldn't they know everything? According to spiritists, spirits aren't omniscient. Plus, they can't always reveal the afterlife's secrets to you. In short, if a spirit refuses to respond, don't get pushy!

O spirit, what grade will I get on my math test?

test

superior
spirits

Superior spirits are the ones to talk to about ethics, how to handle difficult situations, or general questions about society. They enjoy discussing science, history, art, and more. You may even get them to discourse on a book you are reading. Have a pen and paper handy for notes. Who knows, you might get some good material for an essay.

Above all, don't hesitate while communicating. Remember, the spirit world has as many intellectual and character varieties as our world does. Stay alert and try to communicate with the superior spirits, because they're the ones with the good info!

famous
mediums

Before hitting the road in search of fame and fortune as a medium, there are a few more details you should know. Historically it seems that women are predisposed to spirit sensitivity. There have been male mediums, but most of the greats, including the two Fox girls who kicked off the craze, have been girls. Take for instance the case of Eusapia Palladino, who was born in 1854 in Italy. At forty-three, Palladino went on a world tour as a superstar medium. All through France, Italy, Great Britain, Poland, and the United States, Palladino drew famous people and spiritist devotees to her séances. Palladino was a physical medium, and her act involved moving things with the help of spirits. She could lift a heavy pine table four inches off the ground just by laying a finger on it. She could also levitate in the air to the height of the table, or while sitting on a chair, move herself to the table. Witnesses said guitars would spontaneously start playing in the room she was in, and that images of hands or faces formed mysteriously on blocks of paraffin wax or clay, all while Palladino sat with her hands and feet tied to prove that she was not somehow manipulating the images.

Scholars at the time were baffled. They tested Palladino but could not figure out how she did what she did. An astronomer, Camille Flammarion, was so intrigued that he dedicated part of his book *Mysterious Psychic Forces* to his experiences with Palladino. What interested the author most of all were the physical phenomena, for which he sought a scientific explanation.

Daniel Douglas Home

Daniel Douglas Home (1833–1886) was a Scot who could also move objects and spontaneously break glass just by being in the same room with it. He levitated a table to the ceiling and then made it descend, sloooowly. He also levitated himself and would make a hand magically appear. The hand would first arrive as a lump under a tablecloth but would then grab an object and carry it around. If you wanted to shake the hand, just to be polite or to see if anything was really there, you would feel nothing, just empty air! All the witnesses swore that Home was able to produce these incredible effects. Why would they doubt his capabilities as a medium?

Florence Cook

At the end of the nineteenth century, Florence Cook became famous as a medium who could make invisible objects tangible. Her greatest triumph was allowing a spirit named Katie King to appear, take shape, touch people, and play the piano. The spirit would emerge from the medium's mouth while Cook sat as if unconscious. For three years King made appearances until she disappeared for good. The people who saw King were convinced that the experience was real and that they had undeniable proof of the existence of the afterlife.

Pssst...
$1,000
and
I'll appear

Marcelle de Jouvenel

Then there is the eerie case of Marcelle de Jouvenel, a writing medium. She didn't cause guitars to play or tables to float. Her talent was for automatic writing. In other words, she functioned as a typewriter for the spirits—they would use her to transmit messages by guiding her hand as she wrote. The discovery of this talent followed the death of her fifteen-year-old son, Roland, in 1946. In terrible pain and grief, she became convinced that she could still feel her child's presence.

A few months after his death she discovered that she could put a pen on paper and messages from Roland would appear. This went on for twenty-three years! Practically every night, Madame de Jouvenel wrote. Roland, as a spirit, had a lot to say for someone who was on earth for only fifteen years. His preferred topics included God, faith, and his spiritual evolution. His mother collected all his messages in three books.

Could these messages received through automatic writing possibly be real? Do their revelations come from the afterlife? Did Madame de Jouvenel unconsciously write her own thoughts, or was it really her son who dictated these messages to her?

If you still think you might be cut out for a career as a medium, there is one more thing that you should know. According to Allan Kardec, "The medium must consult for free; impartiality is a guarantee of confidence . . . because the capability of being a medium wasn't given to become famous and recognized." In other words, don't become a medium if you think you're going to get rich or maybe host your own daytime television show.

the spirit's responses

spirit, are you there?

tricked!

table-turning

GETTING IN TOUCH

IS IT
DANGEROUS?

table-turning

If you truly want to make a go of spiritism, you'll have to take your meetings seriously. The best thing is to choose a set time and place for your events and keep it consistent. There is no time or day that spirits prefer, no need to wait for Friday the 13th or a full moon. Spirits aren't picky about location either, so you don't need to seek out spooky locales. Consistency is important because the spiritists say that a spirit will leave behind traces of energy after a visit, which will make it more likely to return.

Things to avoid: tacky Halloween-style decorations. As we've seen, spirits are easily offended, and they might find these insulting. You won't need

Pssst . . . a turning
table doesn't count!

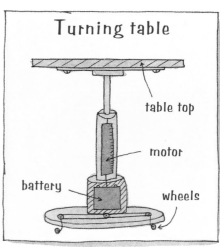

Turning table

table top

motor

battery

wheels

Try one of these:

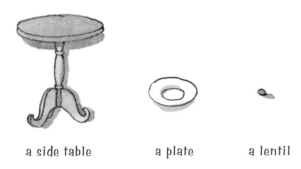

a side table   a plate   a lentil

magic formulas or rituals but you can, according to Allan Kardec, begin each séance like this: "I pray to you, all-powerful God, to allow the spirit of [____] to communicate with us."

Spirits can converse with us using different methods. The table-turning method, considered a practical way of communicating with spirits, spread quickly during the mid-nineteenth century.

How do you make tables turn? The goal isn't to move the table by violently pushing it, but rather to enter into communication with spirits through the table. Take a round table and pose the tips of your fingers on the table's edge. If you don't have a table available, any other circular object (dish, plate, glass, etc.) will work. Once you are situated and able to touch the table, start concentrating, since you have to focus all your energy on the object to make it move. Two kinds of open-mindedness are absolutely necessary. First, you need to be willing to believe, and second, you must clear your mind so that the spirit has room to manifest itself.

Concentrate until you establish a connection of energy between you and the table. The table has to turn only at your command, to the right or to the left. If you succeed after ten seconds, your skills as a medium no longer need to be proved: you're a natural! If it takes you ten minutes, that's not so bad. If the table obstinately refuses to turn after an hour of concentration, don't insist, just go to bed. The spirits either can't or don't want to respond to you, or your physical and mental state won't allow you to do it. Better to try again later.

It becomes far more complicated with a big table

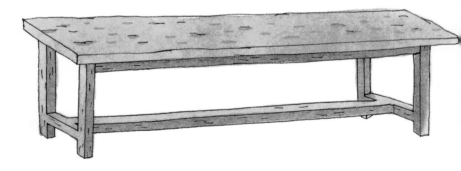

is it
dangerous?

Table-turning is not, physically speaking, dangerous. Do you feel tired and anxious? No worries—it's normal when you're thinking about spirits. In order to make a pine or oak table turn, you don't have to be strong; it's enough to possess an exceptional power of thought. But all that thought takes a lot of energy! If it will make you feel better, get some friends together to practice with you. The number doesn't matter. Nor do you need assigned seating or to alternate boys and girls. No need to hold hands either. Rest only your fingertips on the edge of the table, like on the keys of a piano. Are you ready? Out of respect for the spirit that you are going to call up, absolute silence and complete concentration are necessary. You have to establish a communion of thoughts favorable to the manifestation of spirits, even if, when you communicate through table-turning, it's often those crude, lower spirits who respond. One piece of advice: avoid inviting friends who won't be open to the experience—their negative energy will make it difficult to get things going. When the power of concentration is at its maximum and the communication is well-established, don't be surprised to see the table not only turning but also tilting, rising on one leg, shaking, or lifting off the ground. If it will respond to commands, you've got yourself a spirit!

the
spirit's responses

OK, *you've summoned a spirit* and the table is turning! Now's the time to start asking questions. If the spirit is feeling chatty, it will respond by making one of the table legs rap on the floor: one rap = yes; two raps = no. The language conveyed through rapping, or knocking, is called typtology. There are two kinds of typtology: swinging typtology involves a rapping table leg; interior typtology is when the raps or vibrations are produced inside a wall or the wood of a table. There is always a chance that famished termites have infested your table and are making noise, so make sure you aren't being fooled. If the table vibrates from its legs to its top, the spirit called upon is there! Even really hungry termites can cause only so much vibration.

Once you know you've got a live one, so to speak, you can recite the alphabet aloud: the spirit will rap at the letter that suits him or her and you can construct real sentences: A=1; B=2; C=3, etc. Obviously, it takes a long time; be patient.

You can interrupt the spirit when the word is completed to confirm that you've understood and that this was the word they meant to spell. Some attention-loving spirits will imitate the noise of a saw, a hammer, or a drum, and mark the time or the number of your friends around the table.

No matter who shows up, remember to remain polite and courteous. Spirits, like people, remember who treats them well and will be more likely to show up again if you are kind. You will feel lucky when, the next time you invoke the same spirit, it happily responds—if it has the time—with some intense table-leg rapping!

But don't forget that the superior spirits prefer another mode of communication, automatic writing, and keep in mind the words of Léon Denis, one of the first theorists of spiritism along with Allan Kardec: "If you make frivolous use of spiritism, know that you will become the inevitable prey of lying spirits, the victim of their hoaxes." So, a good word of advice: beware.

ph2

Ooops!
I forgot my pen!

other
techniques

If the idea of turning tables is unappealing, remember the other ways to communicate. You can use what Allan Kardec calls psychography. The spirit communicates through writing, leaving an easily preserved record, like a letter or an e-mail. Of course, automatic writing is the most adaptive procedure since the spirit mechanically guides the arm and the hand of the medium in writing. There is also pneumatography, where the spirit writes without a human intermediary. You can imagine how rare that is. For the beginner, it is best to start with table-turning or playing with a Ouija board; a few people have gotten lucky with more technological approaches. In 1959, near Stockholm, Sweden, Friedrich Jürgensen set out to record some birdcalls, but when he listened to the tape he heard a trumpet playing and a man's voice speaking Norwegian! The messages were incoherent and almost impossible to decipher. However, he had the impression that it had to do with a spirit wanting to communicate with him. The spirit, it seemed, of a trumpet-playing Norwegian. You never know who will show up!

an astonishing
experience

A lot of people at her high school talked about spirits, so Maggie decided to participate in a séance to see if there was anything to the stories. She became interested in the process and started attending regularly. Here is her story:

"My first encounter with the afterlife happened one Saturday night in a dimly lit attic. We were five friends, three girls and two boys. Since I was the only new one, they explained how a séance works and showed me how they did it. They had twenty-six squares of paper on which were written the letters of the alphabet from A to Z, and nine other squares numbered 0 thru 9. The squares were placed in a circle. To separate the letters on one side from the numbers on the other, there were two other squares on each side with YES written on one and NO on the other. All the circles were placed on a round, smooth wood table. On the inside of the shape formed by the squares, there was an overturned glass. The séance was ready to begin!

"Sitting around the table, we placed our index fingers on the glass without pushing down. Then, silence! I felt like laughing, and the others did as well . . . shhhh! Each one of us took his or her turn asking the traditional question that starts each séance: 'Spirit, are you there? If yes, move toward the yes!'"

Sometimes I just use the glass to have a drink of water.

spirit,
are you there?

"We repeated this question as an incantation. I concentrated; I really wanted it to work, just to see, out of simple curiosity. I didn't move at all but I was really excited; I wasn't sure if I was afraid or not! Anyway, I had to concentrate . . . There! The glass moved a tiny bit, I was certain—it moved! I looked at the others; they had also seen it. They motioned to me: above all, stay quiet! The glass moved again, softly, then very distinctly . . . The boy who was overseeing the séance then said, 'Return to the center! The glass obeyed—the spirit was really there! My heart was beating like crazy, but no . . . I couldn't believe it . . . I still had my index finger on the glass,

and the others did as well. The glass moved and responded: 'B.' B? What does that mean? Was it a joke? 'Do you have something you want to tell us?—Yes' . . . The spirit, using the glass, wrote a name: 'Bridget.' There was a girl named Bridget in our class. So we all began to get excited. 'Ask him if it's Bridget M.!' Hesitation from the glass . . . The spirit finally responded yes. So the questions became completely personal: 'Is she going out with Dan?—Yes!' A fit of giggles . . . 'Is it going to last?—Yes!' . . . And the séance quickly degenerated into us gossiping about classmates . . . nobody could concentrate anymore; the séance ended in exhilaration.

"When I went home, I was positive that I had communicated with a spirit, and I was sure that the glass moved all on its own; I was so convinced that I had already agreed to meet up and try it again the following Saturday."

poets,
novelists,
and scientists

conjuring?

tricks and
hallucinations

YOU'RE IN GOOD COMPANY!

FEAR OF
DEATH

poets, novelists,
and scientists

When spiritism first came on the scene, it became a real fad—everyone wanted to communicate with the dead! Poets, novelists, and scientists became fascinated by spiritism séances. Spiritist magazines were launched all over Western Europe and the U.S. In 1927, there were 150 magazines dedicated to spiritism!

Victor Hugo

Among the celebrities of the nineteenth century, Victor Hugo, author of *Les Miserables* and *The Hunchback of Notre Dame*, practiced spiritism. His interest was sparked in the same way that many others came to spiritism, by the death of someone he loved. In 1843, Hugo's twenty-one-year-old daughter, Léopoldine, and her new husband drowned in a boating accident on the Seine. Hugo was crushed. Before starting to practice spiritism, he had written: "Let's believe in God, let's surround him with our obstinate prayers. We will meet our dead again. One day, from here below, we will exclaim: O my God, here they are!"

It doesn't seem surprising then that when Victor Hugo met a medium, Madame de Girardin, who was a specialist in table-turning, he was ready to believe. On September 11, 1853, she organized a first séance at her house, which had a reputation for being haunted. Some people in the neighborhood claimed to have seen a white shadow lurking at night, calling out desperately.

Madame de Girardin couldn't have asked for a better audience than Victor Hugo, who was obsessed with death and with the mysteries of the soul and the world. From the first séance on, he was convinced; he believed Léopoldine's spirit spoke to him. His interest lasted for two years.

The Hugo family started holding the séances themselves. Hugo's son Charles served as medium; Adèle, Hugo's wife, interpreted the messages from the afterlife. Befitting Victor Hugo's status as a great writer, many of the spirits who attended the meetings were writers themselves, like Dante, an Italian poet who died in 1321, author of the *Divine Comedy*.

The spirits dictated poetry and even corrected lines that were interpreted incorrectly. Did Victor Hugo unintentionally influence Charles, or was there, between him and his son, a mysterious transmission of thoughts?

"When we question the table in Charles's absence," Adèle Hugo said one day, "it raps, but only letters without meaning that don't form words. Why?" After two years Hugo decided to stop all communications. It wasn't that he'd lost faith. He'd become concerned that practicing spiritism could have a negative effect on his mental health. His brother Eugène had lost his mind, and Hugo was worried. What he didn't know at the time is that spiritism did seem to have a negative effect on people's minds. The question is, were mentally unstable people drawn to spiritism or was it the practice that caused the problem?

Spirits of
the sea,
I command
you . . .

Théophile Gautier

The author, poet, playwright, and critic Théophile Gautier also let himself get swept up in the whirlwind of spiritism. Many of his short stories deal with the afterlife and mysterious suggestions of the other world.

It makes sense that many romantic poets and novelists of the nineteenth century, like Gautier, would find spiritism compelling. Their imagination made them perfect candidates for exploration of the borders between one world and the next. It wasn't just creative types who got involved, though. What does it mean that spiritism also captured the attention of astronomers like Camille Flammarion, mathematicians like Louis Arago, and physicists like Michael Faraday?

Nineteenth-century science produced new developments in areas that involved "invisible forces" like electromagnetism. As the discoveries regarding magnetic and electromagnetic fields in physics multiplied, the idea that some other invisible force could make tables float and spin became even more interesting.

Camille Flammarion

Camille Flammarion, an astronomer, studied spiritism and felt that it fit right in with being a scientist. He believed that the soul is a real, independent being and the spirit world is as real as the world we perceive with our five senses. In his book *Biographical and Philosophical Memoirs of an Astronomer*, he says the following: "I don't hesitate in saying that he who declares spiritist phenomena contrary to science doesn't know what he's talking about. In fact, in nature, there is nothing mystical and supernatural; there is the unknown, but yesterday's unknown becomes tomorrow's truth."

So what should we believe? Should scientists throw out their telescopes and grab a Ouija board instead? One way to look at it is that scientists of the period did not want to rule anything out.

tricks and
hallucinations

The Larousse Encyclopedia of the Nineteenth Century goes right to the point: "Spiritists suffer from hallucinations and accord a real and objective existence to an imaginary conception of spirits." It states that all spirit manifestations are fraud, pure and simple. What makes it worse is that, according to the Larousse Encyclopedia, mediums often target vulnerable people, like those grieving for dead loved ones.

But what about all that rapping on tables? On September 24, 1888, Margaret and Katherine Fox, the girls who kicked off the whole craze, admitted that it had all been a trick, "the greatest deception of the century." Margaret

said they tricked their mother under the direction of their older sister and it went on from there. Once they started making money, they saw no reason to come clean.

To prove her point, Margaret organized a meeting in which she stood on a table and demonstrated for everybody that the raps had actually come from her cracking her toes. Talk about anticlimactic! How awful, the sounds from the spirit world coming from somebody's toes! Margaret and Katherine Fox ended their days poverty-stricken and alone after revealing the truth.

conjuring?

The medium Daniel Douglas Home was also caught cheating. The spirit's hand that would amaze spectators by brushing against them turned out to be his foot, stuffed into a glove. As if that wasn't bad enough, some people interested in exposing him asked Home to get into contact with some ancestors of theirs. After he did, they revealed they'd invented these ancestors, thus proving Home was making it all up.

Remember Eusapia Palladino? She was undone when a light she didn't know about revealed that she was the one touching the participants at her

séances, not a spirit. And she wasn't moving objects with her mind; she actually pulled objects by tying them to pieces of her hair. In 1880 Florence Cook, the medium who claimed to be able to make spirits appear visible, was also caught in the act. At the moment when she made the spirit of a twelve-year-old girl appear, a spectator went behind the curtain where the medium usually went in order to better concentrate. But no more medium; she had vanished! The chair was empty! Turns out that the twelve-year-old girl was being portrayed by Florence Cook herself.

Tables that turn and levitate, raps, glasses that move . . . are you a victim of your own imagination, or of a trick? When you participate in a séance, doesn't all the concentration put you into an almost trancelike state? A state that makes it a lot easier for you to lose your sense of reality?

I swear to tell the truth, the whole truth, and nothing like the truth—er, wait!

in need
of proof

In 1882, in England, the Society for Psychic Research decided to figure out once and for all if any of this was real. They applied stringent rules to their study and would only accept testimonies of people who had witnessed an apparition or received a message from a friend or close relative within twelve hours of that person's death.

After conducting the study, the society cautiously announced that there may be some cases in which a message does appear to be passed between the living and the dead, but that they could not substantiate many of the claims.

fear
of death

So why would so many people believe in spiritism? The short answer is that there are few concerns more universal than what happens to us after we die. Most of us put our feelings or fear of death to the side. It's a pretty heavy topic to think about all the time. Maybe spiritism caught on to the degree it did because it allowed people access to the fears and desires that they kept locked away. Automatic writing or asking questions of a table are ways to get those questions out there and, maybe more important, to get the answers we want to hear.

Spirits feast on your mind!

and in
other cultures?

Do all civilizations and cultures believe in or try to communicate with spirits? "We consider the soul to be the most important and most mysterious being," said an Igluik Inuit in 1900 to explorer Knud Rasmussen, who directed multiple expeditions in the Arctic. The Igluiks lived in an extremely harsh climate; the physical realities of staying alive could have been the most important concern, but they weren't. What mattered most to the Igluiks was the soul.

For Canada's native peoples, the soul is a small flame that comes out of the mouth. For the Bantus in Africa, the soul separates itself from the body during sleep, visits the souls of the dead, and brings back messages in the form of dreams. So it seems that all over the world people have similar ideas and questions about spirits and the soul. For instance, many diverse cultures use the image of a boat carrying the soul away to the afterlife. In Oceania, the dead cross the ocean to join the sun. In Ireland, the rowboat is the symbol of passage into the next world. And in ancient Egypt, a sacred boat allowed the dead to descend into the underworld to await rebirth.

The rowboat is also what allows an Indonesian shaman—an enlightened person who communicates with the dead, but is also a healer—to travel

Ugh . . . the rowboat is very nice and all, but when can I have the motorboat?

through the air in search of the soul of a sick patient. When the time comes, this rowboat is also what will transport souls to the afterlife. For millions of years, humans have believed that the soul is immortal, even if they have used different images to express the idea. In the *Bardo Thodrol*, the Tibetan book of the dead, which dates from the eighth century, the priest reads a special message to the departing soul: "Don't stay attached to this life because of emotions and weakness. You don't have the power to remain here." Among the Dogon people of West Africa, the dead must be removed from their homes following very specific rules, in order to prevent them from returning to haunt the world of the living. For instance, the body is taken to the cemetery following a route that zigzags all over the place. The idea is that if it is confusing enough, the person's spirit won't find the way back but will stay happily buried!

questions in the
face of death

In most traditional societies, the ability to communicate with the spirit world is handled by a specific person, usually a shaman, who is trained for the job. Why? One reason could be that the intense concentration necessary for communication, even if the communication is within the mind of the shaman, could be overwhelming. It is almost like having a split personality: there is the regular side and the "sensitive" side. Reconciling these two sides can be difficult; the shaman has to have enough control, both to bring on the sensitive state and to end it.

rituals for communicating
with spirits

If almost all societies have rituals for communicating with spirits, does it prove that they really exist? Or does it just emphasize the universality of the desire to control the unknown, whether it is to feel that we can reach out to the people we miss, ask for help when we need it, or receive reassurances?

tasseography

predicting
the future

HUH?

?

to believe or
not to believe
in divination

palm
reading

OTHER BELIEFS
IN THE AFTERLIFE

THE INFLUENCE
OF THE STARS

predicting
the future

In his book *Treatise on Spirit Manifestations,* Allan Kardec claims that every soul has the power to "see without eyes," or to be clairvoyant. How bad could it be, right? Yet in the nineteenth century certain countries passed laws outlawing any kind of fortune-telling. But what do people really want to know about? The future! Will I get into my favorite college, be successful, get married? There are many things to be curious about and almost as many ways of trying to find an answer. All methods of divination, like astrology, numerology, and chirology, respond to the same desire: to feel reassured about our destiny.

Sshh . . . I'm trying to tell you the secrets of your future.

nobody believes in it,

but . . .

Um, astrology? Isn't that, like, completely made up? Are some lines on my palm really going tell me about the future? And what about numerology, where the number of letters in your first and last name gives you info about your talents and abilities. Totally bizarre, right? Maybe. But the weirdest part is that in study after study people consistently say they don't believe it is possible to tell the future, although everyone still wants to try!

A good example of this paradox is the response of a writer who was asked if he believed in ghosts: "No," he said, "but I'm afraid of them!" In other

words, we can tell ourselves all day long that reason proves that things like ghosts and fortune-telling aren't true, but it is harder to shake the feeling that there might be a tiny bit of truth in them.

astrology

One of the most famous ideas handed down to us from the ancient Greeks is the command "know thyself." Figuring out what suits you takes time, but people have traditionally looked to speed up the process one way or another. The Chaldeans are another ancient culture, credited with the invention of astrology; they tracked the location of the planets, stars, and sun at the moment of each of their kings' births. That's exactly what astrology still is: the art of determining one's character and future based on where the stars are when one is born. For a long time, astrology was recognized as a serious subject, and was even taught at universities, handed down more or less secretly from schoolmaster to disciple. Now it tends to be found in the back pages of magazines, but many people still pay attention to their sign and what it might mean for them.

The Chaldeans were the ones who invented zodiac signs. "Zodiac" comes from the Greek word *zodiacos*, which means "wheel of life." The twelve zodiac signs express twelve fundamental structures of the human being. Nature is represented by four elements—fire, earth, air, and water—which are linked to the twelve signs.

The fire signs are Aries, Leo, and Sagittarius, which correspond to energy, animation, dynamism, and a desire for domination and transformation. Scorching!

The earth signs are Taurus, Virgo, and Capricorn, which correspond to stability, obsession, concentration, resistance, and determination.

The air signs are Gemini, Libra, and Aquarius, which correspond to openness, love, communication, and the need for renewal and mobility.

The water signs are Pisces, Cancer, and Scorpio, which correspond to instinct, memory, sensitivity, relaxation, and responsiveness.

The zodiac calendar begins March 21, when the sun starts out in Aries. One month and thirty degrees later, it will enter into the sign of Taurus, and so on and so forth—all of this just to situate your birthday in the zodiac calendar. Since where you were born is also important, astrologers have divided the Earth into twelve sectors, or houses.

the influence of
the stars

An astrological chart, or horoscope, is like a snapshot of the sky at the moment of your birth. The position of the planets in your sign can predict important events in your life or suggest what other signs are most compatible with yours. Most horoscopes play it safe by being extremely vague. The advantage of spiritism over astrology is that ordinary evocations don't require complicated interpretations: Once communication with the spirit is established, each person can directly ask his or her question. Even though we aren't sure who's actually answering!

What's your sign?

palm reading

Three thousand years ago, chiromancy, or palm reading, was already being practiced. The Indians and the Chinese had different techniques for palm reading, while others practiced a Greek method. Chiromancy was popular around the end of the Middle Ages, and some thought it was especially approved of by God, the theory being that if God created every hand, isn't palm reading sort of like getting a divine message? People even pointed to passages in the Old Testament that they thought proved their point.

Your right hand, which probably stays pretty quiet when you look at it, can actually reveal a ton of information. It speaks for you, like it or not, through

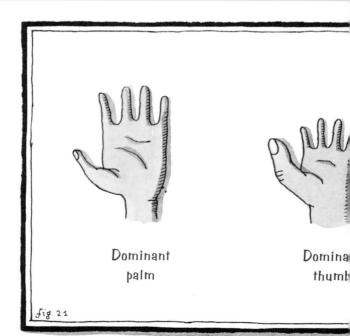

Dominant
palm

Domina
thumb

fig. 21

its shape, through the length of your fingers, through the size of your palm, and of course through the indented grooves formed over the course of the years on your palm. You hold your personality in the palm of your hand! And it's your palm that will be asked all sorts of questions: How do you act? How do others see you? How do you see others? What makes you you? Everything is written in the lines of your palm!

It's the size of the palm and the placement of the thumb and fingers that can provide information to a chiromancer:

- Dominant palm: you are impulsive, you like movement, and you have the ability to take action.

- Dominant thumb: you like order and discipline, you are sometimes authoritarian and not very tolerant,

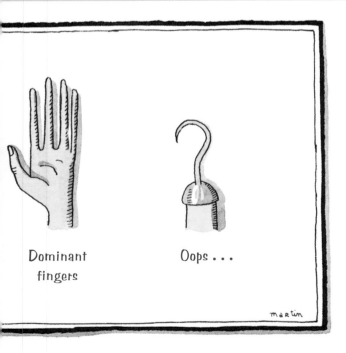

Dominant
fingers

Oops . . .

martin

and you are committed to moral values (such as courage, honesty, and loyalty).

- Dominant fingers: you are at ease in society, stable, and full of self-assurance; you are dependable; always busy, you sometimes feel like shaking up those who hesitate!

Another way of analyzing the shape of the hand emphasizes the nondominant characteristics of the palm, thumb, and fingers.

deciphering
difficulty

To be a good palm reader, you need to study the shape of the palm (round, triangular, or square), the placement of the thumb and fingers (high, low), the length of the fingers, their width, the size of the bones, and of course the lines of the hand.

Before you begin stopping strangers on the street and offering a reading, you need to know what every line means. There are three key lines in chiromancy: the heart, head, and life lines. Then there is an assortment of smaller lines: two important ones are the health and fate lines. Look carefully at your hand: if your fate line (it starts at the wrist and goes until the base of the middle finger) is double, you'll have exceptionally good luck throughout your life. But be careful! Being a good palm reader means being intuitive and sometimes sorting through contradictory information.

numbers

This has nothing to do with telling your future through math problems, does it?! Kind of! It has to do with understanding how numerology, or the science of numbers, is believed to convey information about an afterlife and the future. The difference is, instead of spirits doing the talking, information is revealed by numbers themselves.

Since the sixth century B.C. and Pythagoras, the ancient Greek philosopher and mathematician, people have believed that numbers have a symbolic meaning. Here's how it works: Take your first name and your date of birth, knowing that each letter of the alphabet corresponds to a number from 1 through 9: A = 1, B = 2, etc. When you get to J = 10 you add the two digits together so you always end up with a number between 1 and 9. Got it? To find the numbers of your personality, you add all the numbers up. If your first name adds up to 12 and your last name adds up to 67, you would count it this way: 1 + 2 = 3 and 6 + 7 = 13. Then, because it must be one digit you would add 1 plus 3 to get 4. You can determine your "inner number" by adding the vowels of your last name or your "realization number" by adding up the consonants. The "expression number," the result of your first and last name, indicates the natural tendencies of your character.

According to *The Encyclopedia of Divinatory Arts*, by Catherine Aubier, the expression number system goes like this:

1. independence (I decide)
2. the couple (I partner up)
3. communication (I express myself)
4. effort (I build)
5. movement (I change and travel)
6. feelings (I create harmony)
7. wisdom (I try to understand)
8. strength (I conquer)
9. devotion (I help)

With the help of your date of birth, you can also calculate what your "life path" is. This is more complicated, so before trying it you should get a good manual on numerology. All the difficulty in numerology, as in astrology and chiromancy, lies in the interpretation of the information. What does it mean that your realization number is a 6? A lot of practice in divinatory arts and time spent cultivating psychological intuition and insight are needed to disentangle all this information. Nobody said telling the future would be easy!

cartomancy

Not convinced by the influence of stars, numbers, and lines in your palm? Still having trouble picking lottery numbers? Well, you could try cartomancy, or the art of using playing cards to try to predict the future. The most basic way to do this involves asking a simple question: "Will my wish be fulfilled?" Then there's another, very complex method that gives the person consulting the cards detailed information on his or her past, present, and future. Interestingly, there are as many cards in a deck as there are weeks in a year—fifty-two—and thus four suits of thirteen cards, just like the four seasons.

ph4

Can I pick another card?

Two cards have a meaning in divination: the nine of hearts, the card of success, and the ten of spades, the card of deception. Now, how do you know if your wish will come true? Well, it's actually breathtakingly simple. You can put it to the test any time you have a pack of cards. You draw a card and tap on it while thinking about your wish. Then you give back the card, and the reader cuts the deck and puts the cards down one at a time. If the card of success appears before the card of deception, your wish will come true; if it's the opposite, it won't. Of course, this is more of a game, but some people swear it works!

a positive or negative
influence

Don't forget that hearts correspond—no surprise—to emotions; their influence is advantageous. Diamonds correspond to movement and to news; they have a neutral influence. Clubs mean money. Their influence is positive. Spades signify difficulties and problems and have a negative influence. Cartomancy is a very complex art because cards change meaning depending on their neighboring cards. However, know that in a method of divination involving seven, twelve, or twenty cards, having four cards of the same value always has a particular meaning. For instance, four aces means success for everybody; four jacks means discussions and disputes; four eights means harmony and agreement. But can you rely on all predictions?

tasseography

This one is perfect for lazy people. No need for big preparations, and no need to observe stars and planets: all you have to do is read coffee grounds. All you need is a very dry white cup and saucer. Prepare Turkish coffee by pouring a spoonful of ground coffee into a kettle filled with boiling water. Pour out the liquid coffee, but leave the grounds in the pot for at least an hour. Turn the pot over and dump the grounds in the saucer. Shake the saucer gently back and forth, then pour its contents in the cup, whose handle should be pointed in the direction of the interpreter. It's the patterns left by the coffee ground particles in the cup that will reveal the secrets of your destiny!

So how do you interpret them? Everything in the cup to the left of the interpreter represents past events, and everything to the right, the future.

The image formed next to the cup's handle signifies the coming together of two people, the image formed at the edge of the cup indicates events in the present, and the image formed at the bottom of the cup signifies a serious event to come. But, as always, it's the skill of the interpreter that will make all the difference.

to believe or not to believe
in divination

Having read now about all these methods and practices, the question still remains: *Do I believe? And if so, what exactly do I believe in?* With spiritism, for instance, the two sides are starkly divided. The believers see natural or highly cultivated powers of clairvoyance in mediums, with facts and proof supporting them. The critics see a scam that is useful only for bilking the gullible out of money

Carl Gustav Jung (1875–1961), philosopher and psychologist, believed, on the contrary, that divination shouldn't be looked down upon. He was interested in astrology and in the book of Chinese oracles, the *I Ching*. In the last years of his life, he asked his patients their horoscopes and sometimes even their spouses' horoscopes, too. When people asked why predictions made

To believe
or not
to believe . . .

That is the
question?

through divination often came true, Jung's response wasn't what you would expect: he talked about "synchronicity," or "meaningful coincidence." For Jung, two events that take place at the same time have a connection between them, even if they are perfectly independent of one another. The diviner's talent is that he or she knows how to understand the relationship between them. OK, that seems easier to grasp than spirits coming and telling you to pursue a degree in interior design, but is it really any different? This brings us back once more to the fact that humans, for thousands of years now, will do whatever they can to learn about the unknowable: the afterlife, the present and future, space, and infinity.

spiritism:
a review

The purpose of practicing spiritism is to get in touch with spirits. For some, it's out of a desire to communicate with dead loved ones; for many others it is primarily a way to have fun. The nineteenth-century table-turning craze didn't last. So why do middle and high school students still dedicate Saturday nights to the thrills of the afterlife? Why participate in a séance?

- Is it to respond to an unconscious fear of death?

- Is it only because your friend believes in it, and she drags you there without you really being convinced?

- Because it's interesting?

- Because you have a lot of fun—the group is nice, and with a bit of music, the girls get scared?

- Because this way you have a destination on Saturday nights, and it costs way less than going to the movies?

- Or, quite simply, because you are convinced that you have a level of exceptional extrasensory perception and any minute now your talents as a medium, a soothsayer, or a healer will need no further proof; that you will be on *Oprah*, then get your own show, be recognized on the street; and that, thanks to your vital, energetic, supersensory skills, the horribly tacky vase bought by your grandmother will burst into pieces? (Without you touching it, of course.)

believing in
a better world

So, how can believing in spiritist practices lead to a better world? Remember all that emphasis on superior spirits? These spirits have something to teach us about the afterlife and how we should live on earth. Well, what about religion, which more or less does the same thing? Don't spiritism and religion clash? One of the charges leveled at spiritism is that it tries to rival Christianity by talking about the dead, the afterlife, and resurrection in a different way. For Christians, eternal life begins when they meet God, in the discovery of a pure love. So why would spirits be raising table legs or rapping in walls? Shouldn't they be happily enjoying all that love and leaving our furniture alone? For spiritists, the two ideas coexist; spiritists

You—do you believe in a better world?

feel that the message of spirits is one that certainly works with any belief in God. Allan Kardec described the spirit message like this: "Love God above everything, and your neighbor like yourself. Love one another like brothers. Pardon your enemies; forget insults; banish selfishness, hate, and jealousy from your heart."

What could be bad about that? And yet . . .

danger!

Spiritism has never been unanimously praised. Allan Kardec was certainly sincere in his belief, as were Marcelle de Jouvenel and all those who found signs from the afterlife in automatic writing or in séances.

So, there's really something dangerous? Yes! Absolutely nothing dangerous is going to happen if you are having fun on a Saturday with some friends. Just be aware and set limits. Remember those shamans? Their skill lies in being able to return to normal when the ceremony ends, and you must do so as well. Think about whether what you are hearing is spirits or your own repressed wishes and desires. Your brain is designed in such a way that it can separate dreams from reality and illusion from what is real. Keep your feet on the ground and observe those differences.

Thinking about spirits can be scary because death is scary! It's a worry, and causes a ton of anxiety. And no, it can't be definitively proven that there is a life after death, even if the immense majority of humans on this lovely planet feel deeply that there is. So that concern just adds more apprehension to the subject.

in conclusion

What if, instead of talking about spiritism and table-turning, we talked about spirituality? Maybe the reason spiritism and séances are so attractive is that we crave more than a rational, scientific, computerized world of war, disasters, unemployment, violence, discrimination, and sex? What if séances are really a way for us to articulate our desire for something more elevated? Who wouldn't like to have the certainty that life has meaning, that it doesn't just end? Spirituality is another way to describe the search for a meaning to life and death. Is it discussed on TV? Will it sell things? Have you seen it in an ad? No! Spirituality is another way of seeing things; it demands an effort of reflection, and knowledge of self, others, and the world.

What about thinking of spirituality as a way of feeling alive, not a way of worrying about the dead? Even if it is absurd to be born only to die, even if the deaths of loved ones are horrible, and they should never die because they're loved, what about completely believing that it is necessary "to learn to live and to die, and in order to be a man, refusing to be God," as Albert Camus wrote in *The Rebel*? What if true spirituality meant refusing to worry about an afterlife that is impossible for us to understand and instead choosing to live life to its fullest, as if death will never come?

suggestions for further reading

Books

Harper, Suzanne. *The Secret Life of Sparrow Delaney*. New York: HarperTeen, 2007.

Johnson, Julie Tallard. *Teen Psychic: Exploring Your Intuitive Spiritual Powers*. Vermont: Bindu Books, 2003

Kelly, Lynne. *The Skeptic's Guide to the Paranormal*. New York: Thunder's Mouth Press, 2004.

Netzley, Patricia D. *The Greenhaven Encyclopedia of Paranormal Phenomena*. Farmington Hills, MI: Greenhaven Press, 2006.

Van Praagh, James. *Looking Beyond: A Teen's Guide to the Spiritual World*. New York: Fireside, 2003.

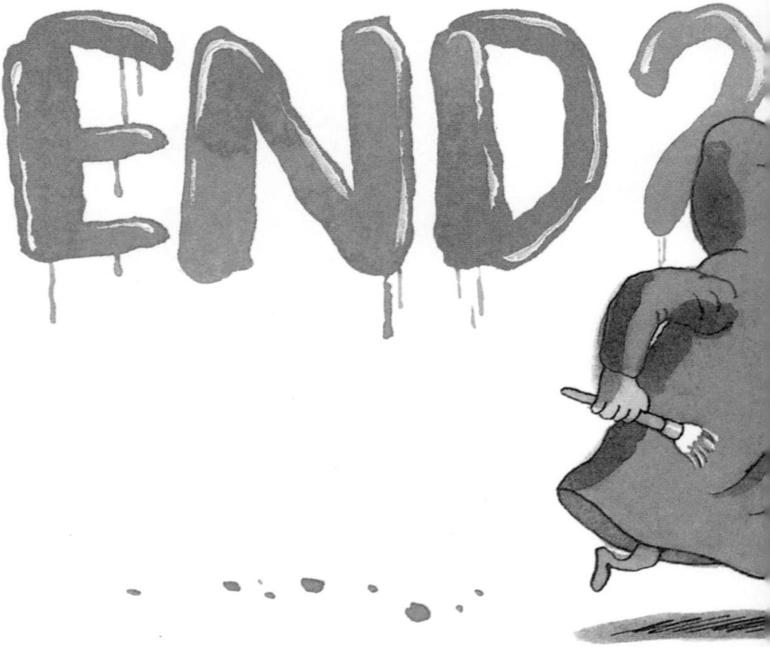
END?